W9-CCP-131

MYSTERY HUNTERS

THE BERMUDA TRIANGLE AND OTHER DANGER ZONES

Sarah Levete

Gareth Stevens
PUBLISHING

...ase visit our website, www.garethstevens.com.
...a free color catalog of all our high-quality books,
call toll free 1-800-542-2595 of fax 1-877-542-2596.

Cataloging-in-Publication Data

Names: Levete, Sarah.
Title: The Bermuda Triangle and other danger zones / Sarah Levete.
Description: New York : Gareth Stevens, 2017. | Series: Mystery hunters | Includes index.
Identifiers: ISBN 9781482460001 (pbk.) | ISBN 9781482460025 (library bound) |
    ISBN 9781482460018 (6 pack)
Subjects: LCSH: Shipwrecks--Bermuda Triangle--Juvenile literature. | Bermuda Triangle--
    Juvenile literature.
Classification: LCC G558.L48 2017 | DDC 001.94--dc23

First Edition

Published in 2017 by
Gareth Stevens Publishing
111 East 14th Street, Suite 349
New York, NY 10003

Copyright © 2017 Gareth Stevens Publishing

Produced for Gareth Stevens by Calcium
Editors: Sarah Eason and Claudia Martin
Picture researcher: Rachel Blount
Designer: Emma DeBanks

Picture credits: Cover: Shutterstock: Maga (t), Triff (r), Tsuneomp (b); Inside: Library of Congress: Edward S. Curtis Collection 39t; Shutterstock: Algol 33t, Vladimir Arndt 23b, Ocskay Bence 42l, Logan Brown 42–43bg, Joel Calheiros 32–33bg, Bonita R. Cheshier 36–37bg, ChiccoDodiFC 12–13bg, Polly Dawson 28–29bg, Doodle 14–15bg, Pierre Jean Durieu 34b, Wojciech Dziadosz 6–7bg, Johan W. Elzenga 19b, Eric Gevaert 32b, Jarvis Gray 34–35bg, Fer Gregory 21t, Chris Howey 38–39bg, Ammit Jack 4–5bg, Subbotina Anna 28b, Another Sun Photography 26–27bg, A Katz 25b, Einat Klein Photography 8–9bg, Vitaly Korovin 10–11bg, Lassedesignen 30–31bg, David W. Leindecker 35c, Lockenes 30t, Olivier Le Moal 11b, Makhnach_S 13b, David Malik 24–25bg, Kazakova Maryia 37r, Mindscape Studio 38b, Oscar Moncho 14t, Mopic 4–5c, Tawin Mukdharakosa 15t, Pratan Ounpitipong 16–17bg, Grigorii Pisotsckii 26b, RCole3 41t, Rweisswald 9t, SevenMaps7 31r, Mark Skalny 40–41bg, Suttisak Soralump 5t, Johan Swanepoel 18–19bg, Taily 16t, Gary C. Tognoni 6b, Triff 1, UMB-O 20–21bg, Kiev.Victor 29t, Joao Virissimo 8b, Marc Ward 20–21b; Wikimedia Commons: 17r, Anynobody 10br, Henry Bowers (1883–1912) 7b, Simon Burchell 25t, dizfunkshinal (http://www.flickr.com/photos/dizfunk/) 27t, NASA/CXC/Stanford/I. Zhuravleva et al 22t, NASA/JPL-Caltech 22–23bg, Nikita Plekhanov 19r, Stephen Reid 43tl, Tony the Marine 40b, US Navy 12c.

Printed in China

CPSIA compliance information: Batch #CW17GS: For further information contact Gareth Stevens, New York, New York at 1-800-542-2595.

CONTENTS

Chapter 1

INTO THE DANGER ZONE

From swirling seas to dusty deserts, Earth can be mysterious, full of wonder and magic—and seriously dangerous. High in the skies and deep underground, our planet inspires awe and amazement. It can also create havoc and fear.

Changing Planet

Scientists believe that Earth formed about 4.6 billion years ago from a cloud of gas and dust. Under the influence of immense forces, the dust and gas gradually took shape as the Sun and the planets of our solar system. Early Earth was a dangerous place, a ball of burning rock. As it cooled, a solid **crust** of rock formed, with a **molten** core. Earth's crust is split into giant plates, called **tectonic plates**, which float on the molten rock beneath. Over millions of years, these moving plates change the shapes of Earth's continents and oceans. The places where the plates rub against each other are **faults**. Earthquakes can happen where plates slide past each other, and burning volcanoes form as molten rock bursts to the surface.

The places where tectonic plates meet are called fault lines.

Discovering Dangers

Many of Earth's most dangerous zones lie along the edges of tectonic plates. These dangerous places are near steaming volcanoes or on shuddering faults. Scientists understand why these places are danger zones. Other danger zones do not have such a scientific explanation, however. Their causes are often far more mysterious.

Read on to find out more about some of the world's most dangerous and mysterious places, and some of the strangest. Find out where you need to tread carefully. Some of the dangers described in this book are very real, but other "danger zones" may be based only on rumor, fear, and **superstition**. It is up to you to figure out which danger zone is real, and which belongs in fiction.

MYSTERY HUNTER

Look for the Mystery Hunter boxes throughout the book. They will ask you to look at the information given in each chapter and answer questions based on what you have read. Then turn to pages 44–45 to see if your answer is correct.

The Valley of Death

Death Valley is the driest and hottest place in North America. Temperatures reach 134 degrees Fahrenheit (57° Celsius) and the valley has less than 2 inches (5 cm) of rainfall a year. Although the searing daytime heat can kill unprepared visitors, Death Valley blooms into colorful flower in the spring! This desert area in Nevada and California was named Death Valley in 1849.

During the Gold Rush (1848–1855) many **emigrants** heading west to make their fortune mining gold in California accidentally found themselves in this desert area. On one wagon train in 1849, 13 emigrants died there. According to **legend**, when they left the desert alive, the pioneers said: "Goodbye, Death Valley." Despite the name, for at least a thousand years, the Timbisha Shoshone Native American community has survived in the harsh region. They learned how to find plants or trap animals that live in the area, and they moved to higher, cooler ground in the scorching summer. Today, many tourists who visit Death Valley think that **Global Positioning Systems (GPS)** and air-conditioned automobiles will keep them safe and cool. However, GPS does not always lead people down safe routes in such a wild region. Only part of the valley has cell phone reception. Over the past 15 years, more than a dozen visitors have perished in Death Valley from heat-related illnesses. Any visitors should take heed of the danger signs.

Death Valley is a place of extreme heat and danger.

Desert of Ice

Antarctica is the windiest, coldest, and driest place on Earth. The temperature can drop as low as −128.6 degrees Fahrenheit (-89.2° Celsius). Antarctica is covered in ice but it is actually a desert! It receives less than 10 inches (25 cm) of rain or snow per year, which is the definition of a desert. Antarctica is similar to the planet Mars: desert-dry and icy cold.

Antarctica is so hostile that only a handful of animals can live there year round. Most Antarctic animals, such as seabirds, whales, and seals, migrate north during the Antarctic winter. Explorers who venture to the icy continent face many dangers. They may become blinded by blizzards, fall into the icy sea, or freeze to death. The most famous disaster to befall Antarctic explorers was when Robert Falcon Scott (1868–1912) and four of his companions died after reaching the South Pole in 1912.

Scott (standing in the center) and his companions all died.

Scorched and Ripped

Around 30 million years ago, boiling, bubbling **magma** pushed up through Earth's crust, causing what is now the Arabian Peninsula to separate from the continent of Africa. Seawater flooded into the **rift** and formed the Red Sea and Gulf of Aden. As the magma cooled, it sank lower. This formed what is now Afar, the East African region of Ethiopia, sitting some 509 feet (155 m) below sea level in parts. Over 30,000 years ago, flooding from the Red Sea left behind huge amounts of salt in a part of the Afar region called the Danakil Depression. Despite scorching temperatures that reach up to 120 degrees Fahrenheit (49° Celsius), Afar people travel there to cut slabs of salt from the ground and load it onto camels to sell at markets. It is one of the harshest and hottest environments in the world.

Danakil Depression

The Danakil Depression was called the "cruelest place on Earth" by *National Geographic* magazine. Not only is it unforgivably hot, with a dusty dry wind, but the land is peppered with volcanoes as the magma continues to bubble and boil beneath the ground. The region also experiences frequent earthquakes. As if this is not dangerous enough, visitors are advised to have armed guards to protect them from rivals battling in the valuable salt industry.

The Arabian Peninsula (center) and the narrow Red Sea to its west formed 30 million years ago.

These camels in Afar cope with harsh conditions.

Ripping Apart Rock

In 2005, a group of Afar farmers were tending their flocks when the ground split apart. They watched in horror as their goats and camels fell into a crack 1,600 feet (500 m) long and 200 feet (60 m) deep. Massive chunks of rock burst out of the ground and a cloud of dust was said to cover the area for three days. Below the surface of the Afar region, the crust is ripping apart. **Lava** from an erupting volcano flowed underground and, as it cooled and hardened, caused the land to crack.

This is terrifying for local people, but scientists believe they are witnessing something extraordinary: the birth of a new sea. Parts of Afar are below sea level, and are cut off from the ocean by only a small piece of higher land in neighboring Eritrea. Over millions of years, rumblings underneath the ground will eventually push away this piece of land. The Red Sea will flood into Afar, creating a new sea.

MYSTERY HUNTER

Based on what you have read in this chapter, do you think there is always a scientific explanation for the deadliest dangers that Earth can present? Justify your answer.

Chapter 2

THE BERMUDA TRIANGLE

Some danger zones are not caused by extremes of climate or landscape, but they are still said to be deadly. They occur on land, at sea, and in the sky, but there is little clear **evidence** pointing to scientific explanations for their reputations. One such danger zone is known simply as the Bermuda Triangle.

The Mystery of Flight 19

"Everything looks strange. It looks like we're entering white water. We're completely lost." On December 5, 1945, the leader of Flight 19—five Avenger planes on a regular three-hour military training mission—sent this alarming radio message to the control tower in Fort Lauderdale, Florida. Within minutes, all five airplanes had disappeared. No trace was ever found of the planes or the 14 crew.

The five planes had left Fort Lauderdale at 2:10 p.m. They were heading toward Abaco Island in the northern Bahamas. Everything was in order. When they set out, the planes had been checked. They had full tanks of fuel. The pilots were well trained, and weather conditions were not unusual. The leader of the training mission, Lieutenant Charles Carroll Taylor, was a very experienced pilot and flying instructor.

Five Avenger planes went missing on December 5, 1945.

A Puzzle

Following the disappearance of Flight 19, experts tried to reconstruct what happened on that December afternoon. They pieced together the available evidence, like completing a jigsaw, but they found there were many key pieces missing. The air crews' conversations over their radios were the most important pieces of the jigsaw. They were overheard by the ground crew and other aircraft in the area. On the radio, at around 3:40 p.m., one member of the crew asked for a **compass** reading. The reply from Lieutenant Taylor suggested that the flight was lost: "I don't know where we are … We must have got lost after that last turn…. Both my compasses are out and I am trying to find Fort Lauderdale, Florida."

Without functioning compasses, Lieutenant Taylor tried to figure out his location by studying the islands below. "I am over land but it is broken," he said. He thought he was over the Florida Keys, but in fact he was way off. Hearing this, staff on the ground figured out the rough location of Flight 19, using **radar**. They were miles from land, north of the Bahamas. The ground staff desperately tried to contact the crew but their messages did not get through, because the weather had grown stormy.

At 6:20 p.m., Lieutenant Taylor was heard to say: "All planes, close up tight …. We'll have to ditch unless landfall. When the first plane drops below 10 gallons [38 liters], we all go down together." That was the final message from Flight 19's five planes.

A compass is an important navigation tool.

Rescue and Loss

As soon as Flight 19 disappeared from the ground crew's radar, they sent several planes and ships out to perform a search-and-rescue mission. Among the rescue planes was a PBM-Mariner **seaplane** with a crew of 13. A few minutes after setting out, the Mariner's pilot called in on the radio to report his location. It was the last call he ever made. Soon afterward, the Mariner vanished from the radar, just as the five Avengers had done. Neither the plane nor its crew was seen again. In one day, six planes had disappeared without trace in the same area.

Did the PBM-Mariner seaplane explode in midair?

MYSTERIOUS FACTS

Examine this timeline of events on December 5, 1945:

- 2:10 p.m. Flight 19 leaves Fort Lauderdale.

- 6:20 p.m. Lieutenant Taylor of Flight 19 transmits his last radio message.

- 7:27 p.m. A PBM-Mariner search-and-rescue seaplane takes off.

- 7:30 p.m. The pilot of the Mariner seaplane radios to say the mission is underway.

- 7:50 p.m. The captain of the ship SS *Gaines Mills* reports a ball of fire in the sky in the region where the Mariner disappeared from radar.

The U.S. Navy investigated the disappearance of the six planes. There were no sightings of the Avenger planes, and nothing to provide the investigators with clues. However, the Navy concluded that the disappearance was caused by Lieutenant Taylor's faulty compasses and human error. Lieutenant Taylor mistakenly thought he was over the Florida Keys, so each change of course he made took his team farther out to sea. In the open seas, there are no landmarks to help figure out where you are. Eventually, all five planes ran out of fuel and plunged into the stormy waters. Evidence from the captain of the nearby ship SS *Gaines Mills* suggested the Mariner seaplane exploded in midair. The Navy stopped building PBM-Mariner planes in 1949. They were known to collect **flammable** gases, sometimes blowing up from a single spark.

Radar uses radio waves to track the movement of planes.

Several planes have disappeared in the Bermuda Triangle.

More Disappearances

After the disappearance of Flight 19 and its rescue plane, there were other reports of missing ships and planes in the same area of the Atlantic Ocean. One of these was a British South American Airways passenger plane, an Avro Tudor IV named the *Star Tiger*. On January 30, 1948, it disappeared without trace, with 31 people on board. No bodies or wreckage were found. Although a report into the disappearance stated, "It may truly be said that no more baffling problem has ever been presented," there were possible reasons for the plane's disappearance. Avro planes had a poor safety record. *Star Tiger* had a faulty heating system and one of its compasses was not working. The pilot may have flown lower in the sky to keep his passengers warm. Flying low uses up more fuel, and makes it hard to avoid crashing if the plane gets into difficulty.

In 1955, a yacht named the *Connemara IV* was found floating in the same area, but without its crew. In 1963, two U.S. Air Force Stratotankers, which are aircraft that carry fuel, also disappeared. These were just a few of the reported disappearances in the region.

It was in February 1964 that the area where these ships and planes were lost became known as the Bermuda Triangle. A journalist named Vincent Gaddis (1913–1997) wrote about the incidents in *Argosy* magazine, arguing that the triangular area of ocean between Bermuda, Puerto Rico, and Miami, Florida, was literally swallowing up ships and planes. Gaddis claimed a **supernatural** force was at work in the area he named the Bermuda Triangle.

The so-called Bermuda Triangle is not marked on official maps.

The Legend of the Mysterious Triangle

A legend grew up about the supernatural power of the so-called Bermuda Triangle. People said that aliens had arrived in spaceships and kidnapped the planes, ships, and crews. Some believe that the lost city of Atlantis is responsible for the strange happenings in the Bermuda Triangle. Greek writer and thinker Plato (428/7–348/7 BC) wrote about an island, named Atlantis, in the Atlantic Ocean that was swallowed up in the ocean waves. Some people believe this island had powerful advanced technology that now creates the dangers of the Bermuda Triangle. And some people also believe that Atlantis was home to aliens! For many people, the name of the Bermuda Triangle continues to conjure up mystery and fear.

MYSTERIOUS FACTS

According to the U.S. Coast Guard, the number of lost ships and planes is no higher in the Bermuda Triangle than anywhere else. Investigation into some of the disappearances leads to possible scientific explanations:

- Hurricanes and storms may be to blame. For example, when the crew of the *Connemara IV* yacht disappeared in 1955, it was the middle of the Atlantic hurricane season.

- Human error and mechanical failure may have caused some plane crashes. For example, many people believe that the two U.S. Air Force Stratotankers that disappeared in 1963 simply collided with each other.

The Devil's Sea

The Devil's Sea (*Ma-no Umi* in Japanese) is an area off the coast of Japan, about 110 miles (180 km) south of Tokyo. You will not find the name "Devil's Sea" written on any official maps. Like the "Bermuda Triangle," the region gained its name only in the twentieth century.

Tales of Loss

According to ancient legend, a huge and hungry dragon used to drag ships to the bottom of the sea off the coast of Japan. In the late 1940s and early 1950s, a number of fishing boats disappeared in the area. The most famous disappearance took place on September 24, 1953. A research ship, the *Kaiyo Maru No. 5*, was investigating an underwater volcano in the area when the vessel and its crew of 31 disappeared. Some people began to be convinced that something strange and supernatural was happening.

Legends tell of fiery sea dragons off the coast of Japan.

Fire Breathers

Scientists have suggested some explanations for the disappearance of ships in the area. The "Devil's Sea" lies over faults in Earth's crust. This has created many underwater volcanoes and there is a great deal of **tectonic activity**, caused by movement of the tectonic plates. Underwater eruptions and earthquakes can create explosions of water and rock, as well as **tsunamis**. Small islands in the area often disappear and new volcanic islands appear.

The *Kaiyo Maru No. 5* was probably destroyed by an eruption of the volcano it was studying, Myojin-Sho. Is it likely that the other missing boats met the same fate? Perhaps the fire-breathing dragons mentioned in the ancient legend were actually volcanoes.

Another possible explanation is that the bed of the Devil's Sea contains large amounts of methane gas. This gas can bubble to the surface around faults in Earth's crust, causing frothy, churning water that can sink unlucky vessels without trace. Some people wonder if the seabed around the Bermuda Triangle also contains large amounts of methane, but this has not been proven.

This photo shows an eruption of Myojin-Sho in 1952.

MYSTERY HUNTER

Based on what you have read in this chapter, what evidence is there that the disappearances of ships and planes in the Bermuda Triangle and Devil's Sea were caused by supernatural forces? Give reasons for your answer.

Chapter 3

DANGER IN SPACE

Look up at the calm night sky. The shining moon and countless glistening stars look so peaceful. But appearances can be deceptive. Space can be very, very dangerous. Remember to duck if you spot a massive rock hurtling toward Earth!

Space Junk

Earth is surrounded by what scientists called "orbital debris"—but what other people call space junk. Humans and their machines in space, such as **satellites**, have created a lot of waste that is no longer used. It needs to be dumped, but there is no waste disposal system in space. The junk just orbits Earth until it crashes to land or collides with something else in space. If some of this debris were to hit the International Space Station (ISS), it could cause terrible damage or even loss of life. The National Aeronautics and Space Administration (NASA) tracks all large space junk and orders spacecraft and the ISS to carry out maneuvers to avoid it if it comes too close.

NASA estimates that one piece of space junk has fallen to Earth every day for the last 50 years. Luckily, no one has been seriously hurt yet. There was a near miss in 2007, when parts of a Russian satellite passed within 5 miles (8 km) of a LATAM Airlines plane carrying 270 passengers across the Pacific Ocean.

Watch Your Head!

Asteroids are pieces of rock that orbit the sun. Sometimes an asteroid can come hurtling toward Earth. Around 66 million years ago, most scientists believe a huge asteroid 6 miles (10 km) wide crashed into Earth. Evidence for this is a 112-mile (180 km) wide **crater** in Mexico. The impact was so powerful that the air was filled with dust, blocking out the sunlight for years. Plants died, followed by many of the animals that fed on them. Nearly all the dinosaurs were wiped out.

An asteroid burned up in the sky over Chelyabinsk in 2013.

This crater in Arizona was made 50,000 years ago by an asteroid about 130 feet (40 m) wide.

Asteroid Attack

In February 2013, a 56-foot-wide (17 m) asteroid traveling at 34,000 mph (55,000 km/h) exploded at 16 miles (25 km) above the ground near the city of Chelyabinsk in Russia. The blast smashed windows in the city, causing mostly minor injuries to more than 1,000 people. If the asteroid had exploded any lower, there could have been much more serious injuries. According to one estimate, there is only a 1 in 75,000 chance of being hit by an asteroid. Even so, NASA has a special department to deal with the threat from Near Earth Objects, including asteroids.

Ring of Radiation

Wherever you are on Earth, you receive **radiation**, or energy, from the sun. Some radiation comes in the form of light and radio waves, which are harmless to us—and useful. Other forms of radiation, such as ultraviolet rays, gamma rays, and X-rays, are harmful to humans in large doses. They can lead to changes in our cells that could cause cancer. Earth's **atmosphere** and its **magnetic field** act like a bubble to shield us from most of the dangers of radiation.

Earth's magnetic field traps dangerous radiation in rings, or belts, thousands of miles above the planet. These are called the Van Allen Belts, because they were discovered by the scientist James Van Allen (1914–2006). The trapped radiation within the Van Allen Belts is dangerously powerful. As spacecraft pass through the belts, computer equipment on board malfunctions, and astronauts report seeing flashing lights, even when their eyes are closed. As long as astronauts pass through the belts quickly, the radiation is not strong enough to damage their body cells.

This illustration shows the magnetic field surrounding Earth. The magnetic field traps radiation in rings around our planet.

Airspace Hazard

There is another problem: the South Atlantic Anomaly (SAA). This is where the inner Van Allen Belt dips down closest to Earth's surface, to a distance of 124 miles (200 km). The SAA is caused by a weak point in Earth's magnetic field. This area is known by some as the Bermuda Triangle of Space. Satellites that orbit Earth have to pass through this patch of extreme radiation regularly, for several minutes at a time.

When it passes through the SAA, the Hubble Space Telescope is programmed to automatically turn off its instruments to prevent damage. The ISS has been given extra shielding to reflect the damaging radiation. In 2016, the SAA is believed to have kick-started events that led to the Japanese Hitomi satellite spinning out of control. The SAA prevented the satellite's direction-finding mechanism from working. The expensive satellite had been launched only 39 days earlier.

Deadly Holes

In space, there are deadly, dangerous holes that suck in anything that comes near them. These are **black holes**. Nothing can escape the pull, or gravity, of a black hole—not even light. Gravity is the force that pulls all matter (or "stuff") toward all other matter. A black hole's gravity is incredibly powerful because a huge amount of matter has been squeezed into a small space. Some black holes begin as giant stars. After millions of years, they collapse in on themselves. The huge amount of matter that was in the star is now squished into a tiny point.

How Big Are Black Holes?

Black holes can be big or small. Scientists think that the smallest black holes may be as tiny as one atom (many times smaller than the tip of a pin), but contain as much matter as a large mountain! The biggest black holes are known as supermassive black holes. These giant black holes lie at the center of most **galaxies**. The supermassive black hole at the center of Earth's own galaxy, the Milky Way, has a mass equal to that of about 4 billion suns and is about 93 million miles (150 million km) across.

Seeing Black Holes

Black holes do not give off any light, so they are invisible to the naked eye. However, scientists can detect them using special X-ray telescopes. As matter is sucked into a black hole, it gives off X-rays. Scientists can also observe the behavior of nearby stars as matter is sucked from the star into a neighboring black hole.

Are We in Danger?

According to NASA, Earth will not fall into a black hole because no black hole is close enough to the solar system. The nearest black hole may be A0620-00, which is 3,000 **light years** away. The sun will never turn into a black hole because it is too small: only giant stars collapse into black holes. However, the sun will eventually run out of fuel and die, swelling up as it does so. This will destroy the solar system's inner planets, Mercury, Venus, and possibly Earth. However, this will not happen for around another 5 billion years, so it is nothing to lose sleep over now.

Chapter 4

WATCH THE HOLE!

Black holes in deepest space may be nothing to worry about, but there are plenty of dangerous holes on Earth. Some you can see, which means you can make sure you do not fall into them. Others simply open up in what looks like solid ground, suddenly swallowing up whatever, and whoever, happens to be passing by. These are called **sinkholes**.

Dune Disappearance

The Mount Baldy sand dune, in Indiana, started to form over 4,500 years ago, when the water level in Lake Michigan dropped about 20 feet (6 m), exposing vast fields of sand to the wind. Today, the mountain of sand is 126 feet (38 m) high. Visitors have often battled with the fierce winds in the area, but now there is another, far more serious, danger to face. Holes suddenly appear in the dune, about 1 foot (30 cm) in diameter. They last for a day or so before being filled with sand again.

In 2014, Nathan Woessner was playing with friends on the dune when he literally disappeared down a hole. It took rescuers over three hours to pull the six-year-old out from the grainy depths. Remarkably, the boy survived the burial in 11 feet (3.3 m) of sand. No one yet knows exactly what causes these sand holes to appear, but we do know that visitors walking on the dune have destroyed much of the marram grass that once stabilized it. More vegetation is being planted on the dune in the hope that it will hold the sand in place.

Deadly Holes

Some sinkholes just cause costly damage to property, but others kill. In 2010, in Guatemala City, Guatemala, an area approximately 65 feet (20 m) wide collapsed about 100 feet (30 m) without warning. It swallowed up a three-story factory, killing 15 people. The sinkhole was most likely caused by the heavy rain from Tropical Storm Agatha and by leaking water from an underground sewer pipe. The water had worn away, or **eroded**, the ground underneath the city.

On February 12, 2014, the United States National Corvette Museum lost some of its precious sports cars. They were not stolen by thieves but literally sank into the ground. A hole 60 feet (18 m) long, 45 feet (14 m) wide, and 30 feet (9 m) deep opened up in the floor of the museum, swallowing up eight very valuable and rare Corvettes. The museum was built on limestone rock, which can be **dissolved** and worn away easily by rainwater.

The Guatemala City sinkhole was caused partly by leaking sewer pipes.

This 20-foot-wide (6 m) and 20-foot-deep (6 m) sinkhole in Brooklyn appeared in August 2015.

Bottom of the World

A group of reindeer herders were walking along in the Yamal Peninsula in Siberia when they nearly fell into the bottom of Earth—or that is how it must have seemed to them. A 260-feet (80 m) crater had appeared where the previous day there had been solid ground. When they peered inside, the herders saw scarred walls leading down to an icy lake 230 feet (70 m) beneath their feet.

Scientists sent down a camera to take images inside the pit. They believe that it was caused by ice melting in the frozen ground. This released gas that built up in pressure. The only way for the gas to escape was by blasting through the ground, leaving a massive hole. Vladimir Pushkarev, the head of the Russian Center for Developing the Arctic, said: "It's an interesting **phenomenon**." Some people believe that there may be other explanations for the sudden crater formation. Perhaps an asteroid smashed into Earth, although there is no evidence to support this. Or perhaps an alien spacecraft crash-landed.

Reindeer herders discovered the crater in Siberia.

Devil's Sinkhole

Watch where you step in Edwards County, Texas. The county is home to a hole about 50 feet (15 m) wide. If you fall down it, you will find yourself in an underground cave 350 feet (106 m) deep, together with huge numbers of flapping Mexican free-tailed bats! During the summer months, watchers on the ground can see millions of bats fly out of the sinkhole to feed. The sinkhole was probably eroded by water. It was spotted by local residents in 1876.

The Devil's Sinkhole is home to more than 3 million free-tailed bats!

MYSTERIOUS FACTS

Here is what we know about how sinkholes form:

- Sinkholes form where water drains belowground and dissolves the rock. Structures on the surface are left on loose soil that can quickly wash away. Some sinkholes form slowly; others form suddenly.

- Human activities such as drilling and construction can cause sinkholes.

- Sinkholes can appear in urban areas when there are poorly maintained water or waste pipes.

- Sinkholes often occur where the rock underground is limestone or gypsum. These rocks are easily worn away by underground streams or rainwater.

especially in Central America, sinkholes filled with water are called cenotes. The water comes from deep underground, so it is clear and pure. Cenotes are common features of the Yucatán Peninsula in Mexico. Hundreds of years ago, this region was the center of the Maya civilization. Cenotes were important to the Maya, who used them as a vital source of drinking water. They built ladders down to the wells at the bottom of cenotes to collect water. The Maya also used cenotes for making **sacrifices** to the gods.

The Maya

Maya civilization developed around 1000 BC and reached its peak around AD 200. Around AD 900, most Maya cities began to decline and were soon abandoned. No one knows for sure what happened to cause the collapse of the Maya civilization, but drought (a long period without rain) and warfare may have been to blame. The Maya had many different gods to whom they offered human and other sacrifices. According to Maya religion, the world had three parts: above the earth (similar to heaven), the earth, and below the earth (similar to hell). **Archaeologists** believe that the Maya made sacrifices to their rain god, Chaac, in **sacred** cenotes.

There are about 7,000 cenotes in Mexico's Yucatán Peninsula.

30

The Sacred Cenote at Chichén Itzá was used for human sacrifices.

Remains of the Dead

From 1904 to 1910, the archaeologist Edward Herbert Thompson (1857–1935) explored the Sacred Cenote at the Maya city of Chichén Itzá. The city was built around a cluster of cenotes that provided the citizens with water. Thompson sent divers into the cenote. The divers were putting their lives at risk: swimmers in cenotes can easily become entangled in tree roots and vegetation. Before they lower themselves into a cenote, divers often perform a ceremony to ask the gods for permission to enter. According to legend, a large serpent with a horse's head protects cenotes, and will grab any child who gets too close.

Thompson's brave divers found pottery and precious goods such as jade and gold. They also discovered the remains of animals and humans. The human skulls and bones belonged to babies, children, teenagers, and adults. Wounds found on the bones suggest that these people were human sacrifices.

The Door to Hell

For more than 40 years, a roasting fire has been blasting out heat from a vast hole in the ground in the Karakum Desert in Turkmenistan. If anything gets too close, it is burned to cinders. This is the Darvaza Gas Crater, although it is more often called the Door to Hell. What created this blazing inferno?

The Darvaza Gas Crater has burned for over 40 years.

In 1971, **geologists** were drilling in the desert, on the lookout for oil, when they broke into an area filled with natural gas. The ground beneath their drilling equipment collapsed, sending it hurtling into a pit. The geologists were left facing a gaping hole about 225 feet (70 m) wide and 98 feet (30 m) deep, filled with flammable and poisonous gas. They decided to get rid of the gas by burning it off, thinking it would be gone in a few weeks. Instead of burning itself out, however, the gas continues to flame away, lighting up the landscape! However, not everyone believes this official explanation of events. Some people think something sinister and as yet unexplained caused the Darvaza Gas Crater. Some local people wonder if it really is an entrance to hell.

The Gateway to Hell

In 2015, a fiery hole opened up on a mountainside in northwestern China. Frightened locals named the hole the Gateway to Hell. Construction workers near the city of Ürümqi were amazed when they came across the pit, which had started to pour out fumes. Inside the hole, temperatures reached a remarkable 1,458 degrees Fahrenheit (792° Celsius). The escaping fumes were so hot that tree branches burst into flames when held over the hole. Scientists are still trying to figure out what caused the pit to open. The area beneath the hole was used as a coal mine in the 1970s. It is possible that some of the remaining coal burst into flames.

Did supernatural forces cause the fiery hole at Ürümqi?

MYSTERY HUNTER

Based on the information you have read in this chapter, what scientific evidence is there that sinkholes are caused by natural forces? Give reasons for your answer.

Chapter 5
DANGEROUS WATERS

About 70 percent of Earth's surface is covered by water: rivers, oceans, and lakes. Much of the deep oceans (containing over 95 percent of the planet's liquid water) remains unexplored. Until scientists are able to reach the depths of the vast oceans, many of their mysteries will remain unsolved and their dangers unpredictable.

Most Dangerous Seas

According to a 2013 study carried out by the World Wildlife Fund, the most dangerous seas and oceans are the South China Sea, the eastern Mediterranean Sea, the Black Sea, and the North Sea around the British Isles. Ships are most likely to have accidents in these seas. They are danger zones partly because these waterways are very busy with shipping. Accidents are also often caused by poorly maintained or aging ships.

However, researchers also say that climate change is causing more frequent and violent storms, which is adding to the risks sailors face at sea. On average, two ships sink every week, somewhere on the world's oceans. Every year, 2,000 seafarers die on the oceans.

Climate change is increasing the dangers faced by ships at sea.

Missing Crew

The oceans hold the key to many unexplained mysteries. On November 7, 1872, a ship named the *Marie Celeste* set sail from New York for Italy. It was captained by Benjamin Spooner Briggs. On board were Briggs's wife and daughter, and a crew of seven. On December 4, the crew of another ship spotted the *Marie Celeste* floating toward them. There was no sign of life, so the captain ordered some of his crew to board the ship.

The abandoned Marie Celeste *was spotted on December 4, 1872.*

The lifeboat was missing and there was some water in the ship, but it was otherwise sound. There was six months' supply of food on board, and the crew's belongings—but no sign of the 10 people. There have been many theories about why the ship was abandoned. Some people say the crew was taken by pirates or abandoned the ship in stormy seas. Some even suggest they had been eaten by a sea monster. To this day, no one has solved the mystery of the *Marie Celeste*.

Rogue Waves

One terrifying ocean phenomenon can put even the largest passenger ships at risk. A ship may be sailing across the calm ocean when suddenly a giant wall of water appears as if from nowhere. Fishermen have long told tales of giant waves appearing without warning, but now scientists have used a mathematical equation to explain how such massive waves can erupt. They can be caused by a combination of winds, **swells**, and **currents**. The existence of rogue waves, over 80 feet (25 m) high, has been proven by photographs and radar. In 2014, the *Marco Polo* cruise ship was struck by a rogue wave in the English Channel between England and France, killing an 85-year-old man who was sitting indoors in the restaurant.

Strange and Dangerous Lakes!

The calm water of Lake Natron in Tanzania looks refreshing, but drinking it would be very unpleasant. Lake Natron has an extremely high alkaline content caused by sodium carbonate and other **minerals** that flow into the lake from the surrounding hills.

This means the water can burn the skin and eyes of animals that are not used to it. However, the lake is home to countless animals, such as flamingos, that are used to its strange water. The strangest of all the water's qualities is that, when an animal dies in the lake, deposits of sodium carbonate help preserve the animal's body, making it look like a hardened shell. Sodium carbonate was used in Egyptian mummification.

These flamingos can brave the burning waters of Lake Natron.

The Blue Lagoon in Derbyshire, England, used to be a popular destination in the summer months. The beautiful blue pool was in an unused **quarry**. However, its beauty was only on the surface. The water contains car wrecks, garbage, and sewage. Swimming in it can cause severe upset stomach. In 2013, the local government took the step of dying the water black to stop people from wanting to take a dip.

Polluted waters pose a danger to humans and wildlife.

MYSTERIOUS FACTS

Here are some of the world's most polluted waters:

- India's Ganges River contains human sewage, factory waste, and dead bodies. Millions of people use the river for drinking, bathing, and cooking.

- Currents in the Pacific Ocean drive plastic waste into an area called the Great Pacific Garbage Patch. It covers 5.8 million square miles (15 million sq km).

Boiled Alive

The "Boiling River" in Peru is said to be so hot that it kills anything unlucky enough to fall into it. That sounds like a **myth**, but could there be any truth in the story? Scientist Andrés Ruzo heard about the river from his grandfather, who told him the traditional tale of how Spanish invaders found the boiling waters when they tried to drown an Inca emperor. The Incas had built a civilization in Peru before the Spanish conquered the region in the sixteenth century.

A Painful Death

Ruzo was determined to find out if the Boiling River really existed. He had to travel deep into Peru's Amazon rain forest to find it. In the Mayantuyacu area is a river that local people call "Shanay-timpishka," which means "boiled with the heat of the sun." The river is about 5.5 miles (9 km) long. Its waters reach temperatures of 200 degrees Fahrenheit (94° Celsius). For any unfortunate creatures that fall in the river, death is not pleasant. According to Ruzo: "The first thing to go are the eyes. Eyes, apparently, cook very quickly. They turn this milky-white color. The stream is carrying them. They're trying to swim out, but their meat is cooking on the bone because it's so hot. So they're losing power, losing power, until finally they get to a point where hot water goes into their mouths and they cook from the inside out."

Could the heat of the Boiling River come from hot springs heated by magma inside Earth?

Sacred River

The Boiling River is considered a sacred place by the local community. According to local legend, its heat comes from the river's giant serpent spirit. A more scientific theory is that the heat comes from fault lines in Earth. The water is heated underground by red-hot molten rock. Discovering the river, Ruzo says, "has forced [him] to question the line between known and unknown, ancient and modern, scientific and spiritual. It is a reminder that there are still great wonders to be discovered." Ruzo has set up the Boiling River Project to research the river, and to protect it and the surrounding area.

Is the sacred river's heat caused by a serpent spirit?

MYSTERY HUNTER

Based on the information you have read in this chapter, do you think that the greatest dangers on the world's waters are caused by humans or by nature? Give reasons for your answer.

Chapter 6

TALES OF DANGER

Many tales of dangerous places may be based on facts, but over time the stories can become exaggerated and made far more incredible. As people retell accounts that they have heard, they sometimes add details that are not accurate. Often it is hard for a mystery hunter to figure out what is fact and what is fiction. This is particularly true when an event took place a long time ago.

Village of the Missing

According to legend, in 1939, a Canadian fur trapper named Joe Labelle passed through Anjikuni, an **Inuit** village that he knew well. About 25 men, women, and children lived in the village on the shore of Anjikuni Lake in Nunavut, Canada. Labelle was expecting the usual warm and friendly greeting from the villagers. However, there was nothing. Literally.

According to reports of what Labelle said, the village was deserted. The villagers' kayaks (boats) were there, as were their hunting rifles and food. But there were no people.

According to legend, even the village sled dogs were dead.

Alarmed, Labelle is said to have alerted the Mounties, the Canadian police, who set up a search. They found no trace of the villagers. To their horror, however, they discovered that a grave in the village had been dug up. They also found the dead bodies of seven sled dogs buried deep under the snow. Inuit villagers from nearby reported seeing blue lights.

Is the Story True?

This is the story according to the legend that has grown up around Labelle's account. However, evidence later emerged to suggest that Labelle had never actually been to the village before. There is little evidence to prove his account of the story.

Could an entire Inuit community really have disappeared?

Evidence from the time is very difficult to find, so researchers try to piece together and check the scraps of evidence that do exist. One photograph that accompanied an article about the mystery showed an abandoned-looking village. The photograph was not from the village in question, however. Reporters had used it to help make the story seem more believable. Some people believe the whole account was a **hoax**. Others think the story was exaggerated and grew up from a less sensational account involving a much smaller number of people. The Mounties have no record that the incident ever took place.

Superstition Mountains

The Superstition Mountains are a mountain range in Arizona. They stretch across 160,000 acres (64,000 ha) of desert, rising to heights of 5,000 feet (1,500 m). The mountains have volcanic peaks and ridges, and boulder-filled canyons. Mountains can be dangerous places for climbers who are unprepared for the weather conditions or the physical demands of the climb. It is not unusual for people to die on mountains. However, the Superstition Mountains are said to have claimed many lives in mysterious circumstances. Some people believe that the mountain range is subject to supernatural forces over which humans have little control.

Pathway to Hell

In some Native American traditions, large mountains are sacred. According to local Apache myths, the hole leading to hell lies in the Superstition Mountains. The wind blowing from this hole creates the many dust storms in the area. The mountains' English name comes from early European settlers, who heard about the legends and stories from Native Americans.

Lost Dutchman's Gold Mine

Some people believe that a lost gold mine is hidden in the Superstition Mountains. The stories say that the mine contains massive amounts of the precious metal. Thousands of people have tried to discover the hidden mine, without success—but that has not stopped people from trying. Since the late nineteenth century, several people have died in the search, including three hikers who died in extremely hot weather in 2010.

The lost mine takes its name from a German ("Deutsch," meaning German, sounds like Dutch) named Jacob Waltz. He may have been a real person who lived in the nineteenth century. He is said to have found the mine and kept its location a secret, but this account is disputed.

Did Jacob Waltz take his secret to the grave?

The Story of Adolph Ruth

According to one story, a treasure seeker named Adolph Ruth was given an ancient map showing the location of the mine in the Superstition Mountains. In 1931, Ruth, an old man, set off to find the mine. He never returned. His skull was later found with two bullet holes in it. There was also a note written by Ruth saying he had found the mine. The map was gone.

Some believe that Weaver's Needle peak points to the location of the mine.

Natural Wonders

There are many myths that explain how Earth's wonderful places came to exist. These are often stories of danger, adventure, heroes, and gods. Even today, when there are good scientific explanations for most natural wonders, people often continue to believe the myths—or at least parts of them.

Eruption!

Can you believe that an ancient volcanic eruption could create 40,000 interlocking rock columns that fit together almost perfectly, like jigsaw pieces? It is hard to believe, but that is the scientific explanation behind the Giant's Causeway in Antrim, Northern Ireland. About 60 million years ago, a volcano erupted in the area. As the lava cooled, it shrank and cracked. These cracks are what form the incredible rock pieces in the Giant's Causeway.

Were the blocks of the Giant's Causeway created as lava cooled and cracked?

Battle of the Giants

There is an alternative explanation for the creation of these remarkable columns of rock. According to Irish myth, an Irish giant named Finn MacCool was challenged to a fight by a Scottish giant named Benandonner. Scotland lies across the Irish Sea. Finn took on the challenge. He used rocks to build a causeway, or track, so he could cross the sea to fight his enemy. According to one version of the story, when Finn reached Scotland and saw the size of mighty Benandonner, he took fright and ran back to Ireland, breaking up the causeway as he went. This legend explains why there are similar columns on the Scottish island of Fingal's Cave.

Fascination and Fear

Earth is a mysterious and wonderful place. Humans have discovered some of its secrets and mysteries, but not all of them. We understand the danger posed by some of Earth's wonders, but there are others that continue to inspire both fascination and fear. The mystery hunter's task is to search for the truth, however strange it seems.

Did Finn MacCool build the Giant's Causeway?

MYSTERY HUNTER

Based on what you have read about the Superstition Mountains, do you think there is enough evidence to prove that they have supernatural powers? What do you think could have led to the deaths of the treasure seekers? Give reasons for your answers.

MYSTERY HUNTER ANSWERS

Chapter 1

Q *Based on what you have read in this chapter, do you think there is always a scientific explanation for the deadliest dangers that Earth can present? Justify your answer.*

A Extreme cold and heat, volcanic eruptions, and the movement of tectonic plates present great dangers to humans, but scientists can explain them all. Scientists also continue to make discoveries that improve our understanding of the natural world, including violent changes in the landscape. However, until there is a scientific explanation for all of Earth's unusual features, humans will often attribute them to strange and mysterious causes.

Chapter 2

Q *Based on what you have read in this chapter, what evidence is there that the disappearances of ships and planes in the Bermuda Triangle and Devil's Sea are caused by supernatural forces? Give reasons for your answer.*

A There is no evidence to conclude that the missing ships and planes in either the Bermuda Triangle or Devil's Sea are caused by supernatural forces. More evidence points toward other causes, including human error, mechanical failure, bad weather, and volcanic activity.

Chapter 3

Q *Based on what you have read in this chapter, which event or activity in space do you think presents the most danger to humans? Back up your answer with scientific evidence presented in this book.*

A One of the most likely dangers to astronauts comes from space junk. Black holes are deadly to anything that comes within their orbit, but it is unlikely that Earth will come close to one. On Earth, the greatest danger comes from space rocks such as asteroids. However, agencies such as NASA are constantly checking for possible asteroid collisions.

Chapter 4

Q *Based on the information you have read in this chapter, what scientific evidence is there that sinkholes are caused by natural forces? Give reasons for your answer.*

A There is significant scientific evidence to prove that sinkholes are caused by natural activity in the ground. When excess water seeps underground, it can dissolve some rocks. This weakens the support on which the surface layer of earth sits, causing sinkholes. However, there is also evidence that human activities, such as construction and poor maintenance of pipes, can contribute to the formation of sinkholes.

Chapter 5

Q *Based on the information you have read in this chapter, do you think that the greatest dangers on the world's waters are caused by humans or by nature? Give reasons for your answer.*

A The sea is an unpredictable force, with storms and rogue waves. These remain the greatest threats to human lives at sea. However, human activities contribute to global warming, which may be increasing the dangers of the ocean. Crossing the seas in ships that are neither properly equipped nor seaworthy increases risks. Human activity has also led to pollution, which makes some lakes and other bodies of water dangerous.

Chapter 6

Q *Based on what you have read about the Superstition Mountains, do you think there is enough evidence to prove that they have supernatural powers? What do you think could have led to the deaths of the treasure seekers? Give reasons for your answers.*

A A number of people have died searching for the lost gold mine. However, there is no evidence to suggest their deaths were caused by supernatural powers. It is likely that most of their deaths were due to the difficulties of coping with the landscape and climate. Adolph Ruth was killed by bullets rather than supernatural forces. However, superstitions and legends about the mountains will continue to be told for as long as people enjoy tales of mystery, gold, and adventure.

GLOSSARY

archaeologists people who study the past by examining ruins and artifacts

asteroids space rocks

atmosphere a layer of gases that surrounds a planet

black holes areas in space with huge gravity that pulls everything toward them

compass a device with a pointer that shows the direction of magnetic north

crater a massive hole caused by volcanic activity or an asteroid crash

crust the solid outer layer of Earth

currents bodies of water moving in one direction

dissolved became part of a liquid

emigrants people who leave one place to live in another

eroded worn away

evidence facts that can prove the truth of something

faults cracks in Earth's crust

flammable easily set on fire

galaxies systems of millions of stars

geologists scientists who study Earth

Global Positioning Systems (GPS) navigation systems that work with satellites orbiting Earth

hoax a trick

Inuit the indigenous peoples of Arctic North America

lava molten rock from a volcano

legend a traditional story

light years measures of the distance traveled by light in one year

magma liquid rock below Earth's surface

magnetic field an invisible area where an object has a magnetic influence

minerals naturally occurring substances

molten melted to a liquid by heat

myth a traditional story that explains a natural event

phenomenon a strange event

quarry a hole dug during mining

radar a system to detect the presence of objects using radio waves

radiation energy that travels as waves or particles

rift a crack or break

sacred holy, or connected with the gods

sacrifices offerings to the gods, sometimes including animals or humans killed for the purpose

satellites objects that orbit Earth

seaplane an aircraft designed to take off from and land on water

sinkholes holes in the ground caused by collapses of the surface layer

supernatural a force for which there is no scientific explanation

superstition belief in the supernatural

swells areas of ocean waves caused by a weather system

tectonic activity earthquakes and volcanoes caused by movement in Earth's crust

tectonic plates moving parts of Earth's crust

tsunamis massive waves

FOR MORE INFORMATION

BOOKS

Athans, Sandra K. *Secrets of the Sky Caves: Danger and Discovery on Nepal's Mustang Cliffs.* Minneapolis, MN: Millbrook Press, 2014.

Bingham, Jane. *The Bermuda Triangle* (Solving Mysteries with Science). North Mankato, MN: Raintree, 2013.

Levete, Sarah. *Science Fact or Fiction? You Decide!* New York, NY: Crabtree, 2010.

Treinish, Gregg and Kitson Jazynka. *Danger on the Mountain: And More True Stories of Extreme Adventures* (NGK Chapters). Washington, DC: National Geographic Children's Books, 2016.

WEBSITES

Check out this website for fascinating information on the Maya civilization:
kidskonnect.com/history/ancient-mayan

This encyclopedia offers information on planet Earth and its formation:
www.q-files.com/earth

NASA's official site presents information about space exploration:
www.nasa.gov

Find out more about sinkholes here:
www.weatherwizkids.com/?page_id=1331

INDEX